I Thought There Was a Road There...

and Other Lessons in
Life from God

Lynn Assimacopoulos

I THOUGHT THERE WAS A ROAD THERE
Copyright © 2023 by Lynn Assimacopoulos

ISBN: 978-1639455850 (hc)
ISBN: 978-1639455843 (sc)
ISBN: 978-1639455867 (e)

Library of Congress Control Numbers: 2023905923

All rights reserved. No part of this publication may be reproduced, distributed, or transmitted in any form or by any means, including photocopying, recording, or other electronic or mechanical methods, without the prior written permission of the publisher, except in the case brief quotations embodied in critical reviews and other noncommercial uses permitted by copyright law.

The views expressed in this book are solely those of the author and do not necessarily reflect the views of the publisher, and the publisher hereby disclaims any responsibility for them.

Writers' Branding
(877) 608-6550
www.writersbranding.com
media@writersbranding.com

Table of Contents

Dedication

Chapter 1: "I Thought There Was a Road There." 1

Chapter 2: The Ride of My Life 5

Chapter 3: One by One 11

Chapter 4: Surprise, Surprise 15

Chapter 5: The Disappearing Fence 19

Chapter 6: Midwestern Sharks 23

Chapter 7: The Homeless Man and the Brainless Woman 27

Chapter 8: When I Lost the Need to Know 31

Chapter 9: The Struggle 35

Chapter 10: To Be or Not To Be...a Sheep 39

Chapter 11: The Future is Coming 43

Chapter 12: Stuck Where I Did Not Belong 47

Chapter 13: My Mother, God, and President Truman 49

Chapter 14: Up the Down Gangplank 53

Chapter 15: A Nosey Risk 57

Chapter 16: A Shiny Secret Place 61

Chapter 17: Making It Complicated When It Is Not! 65

Chapter 18: Taking It From the Top...like "Tigger" 69

Chapter 19: Life After the Carnival 73

Chapter 20: Ducks, Ducks Everywhere 75

Chapter 21: That was Enough of That! 79

Chapter 22: Messages I Did Not Want to Get 83

Epilogue 87

Dedication

This book is dedicated to my husband, Costas, and our three sons, Aris, Paul and Chris who have all provided me with an abundance of lessons in life, each one in their own individual way. It is my hope that I have learned and used these lessons well.

Chapter 1

"I Thought There Was a Road There."

When one of our sons first learned to drive at age 14, he was allowed by law to have a restricted license, which meant he could only drive until eight o'clock at night. Of course, he was excited even at that. And he always showed up only a few seconds before or after 8 p.m. One night he still was not home by then. At 8:15 the phone rang. He and a friend were riding around and had become stuck in a snowbank near an elementary school at the other end of town. They were all right but could not get the car to budge.

I rushed there in a mother-like frenzy and arrived to see the small red car nose-down in a very large snow bank in the middle of the school playground. Our son and his friend were sitting in the front seat just laughing their heads off. I, on the other hand, was NOT laughing.

When I approached, after walking through several feet of snow, my first question was *"How on earth did the car get here in the middle of this playground?"* Then came the words I will never forget. They were *"I thought there was a road there."*

Needless to say I was not happy with that answer and repeated those words several times in disbelief!

> *"You thought there was a road there?"*
> *"Do you see any road signs there?"*
> *"Do you see any street lights there?"*
> *"You thought there was a road there?"*

The boys were no longer laughing. We had a very silent ride home and I told our son he needed to call the tow truck company, to explain to them where the car was and to be there and pay the bill when the tow truck pulled the car out.

When the tow truck guy came, I expected him to be at least as outraged and appalled at this incident as I was. But he was not. He was very calm, smiled and said he had been through many of these. He had teenagers himself and there was nothing that surprised him. Our son should have thanked him for calming me down. As it turned out, our son and his son became good friends a few years later and we all had a few good laughs about his line... *"I thought there was a road there."*

When I was 13 years old, I found an ad in the back of a magazine. It had a picture of a woman's head and the words "DRAW ME." Instructions stated if you drew it well and sent it in to the company you could win an art course and "become a famous artist". I practiced and practiced, drew the picture and sent it to the company. Several weeks later, I was notified by mail that I had won the "honor" of taking this wonderful art course through correspondence and could "become a famous artist"! Then a salesman showed up at our house to sign me up as the winner. It would only cost my mother a few hundred dollars. I thought there was a road there...but my mother assured me there was not!

When I was 18 I didn't want to go to college. I wanted to join the Navy and see the world and travel to exotic places. I had already made the appointment with the Navy recruiter. My uncle, who had been through a career in the Navy, got wind of this (I suppose from my mother).

I thought there was a road there...but my uncle convinced me there was not!!

Many years ago my husband got a very exciting job offer in a small, but beautiful West Coast town. No winter, sunshine every day and close enough to drive to the ocean in an hour or so. I gave away all my winter clothes and prepared to live in "paradise." It turned out it was a very miserable town to live in and we moved from there one year later. We thought there was a road there...but roads seldom lead to paradise.

I once got a bright idea I was going to get an MBA degree. I could go to night school and take other courses through correspondence. So I decided I would take accounting first, through correspondence.

I Thought There Was a Road There

This course couldn't be so hard, I surmised. In fact it most likely was very simple. I thought you just put income on one side of a page and expenses on the other. Simple! Just like my checkbook. Then I received the textbook in the mail. It was at least 6 inches thick. Not so simple, I decided. In fact, it seemed to me it was written in another language. I lasted 3 weeks. I thought there was a road there... but there was no road for me there!

I am certain I will fall again into this "thinking there is a road there" scheme life seems to hand me sometimes. I am also pretty certain I am not alone in this experience. Isn't it true that we as human creatures, many times think there is a road here...or there...and many times we are misled or mistaken?

I have several of what today are called "FAST MAPS." They are plasticized and will not rip. You can read them pretty fast. I have fast maps of cities, states and a fast map of the whole United States. I like these fast maps. I do not want to waste any time trying to fold and unfold a map, and trying to look for the right road and trying to decide which way to go. I want the fast way, the fast road. Most of us do want the fast road. The fast road to riches, to fame, to luck, to getting material things, to have people like us, to make us feel good, to get rid of problems. However, this is not always the case nor the wisest wish. As our son was, we sometimes are mistaken. And we are so tempted to start down that road no matter what the cost or consequences. And we get stuck, nose down, and have to be pulled out. The consequences of the red car having to be pulled out were very minor compared to the consequences on the human soul and spirit when we always insist on taking the wrong road or the fast road.

***

However, God is always on stand-by waiting for our call from *"I-Thought-There-Was-A-Road There"* land to come with a Spiritual Tow Truck, to pull us out. He does not ask in a loud, angry voice, *"Did I tell you there was a road there?"* or *"Did I give you any signs that you should go on that road?"* or *"Did you see any of my shining light down that road?"* No, He probably just shakes his head, keeps calm, pulls us out, smiles and hopes we can muster up enough sense to go in the right direction next time.

Chapter 2

The Ride of My Life

One summer vacation, I made a big mistake. I allowed my husband and our three sons to talk me into going horseback riding on a trail. I had never been on a horse in my life. Nor did I ever want to. Horses scare me. They look at you funny like they know something you don't.

This vacation, I was talked into getting on a horse.

"It would be fun." they said.

"What if the horse bucks and I fall off?" (I wanted to add *"and I break both legs and both arms and I am in a full body cast and you all have to get your own meals and buy the groceries and run errands and wash and iron clothes and clean the house."* but I didn't. I was trying to be a good sport.)

The trail leader assured me he would give me the most gentle horse of the group and he had never had a horse buck anyone. So I relented. And that was my big mistake.

The horse he brought out for me may have looked gentle but it was very big and very tall. About 16 feet tall it looked to me. How on earth was I going to get on this horse using only one little stirrup on the side? Well, it took four people to do it but they got me on the horse!

I still do not understand why there is only one little knob on the saddle to hang onto. I wanted handles or a sturdy bucket seat with a seatbelt or even one of those big baskets which are put on top of elephants. So there I sat wondering why I was doing this in the first place. But I was too embarrassed to say I changed my mind. Besides, then everyone else would have to get off their horses so they could help me get down. So I just sat there wishing I was not up there.

Since the trail leader knew I had the most gentle horse and the slowest horse, he placed me at the very end of the trail line. I was glad because then I could grumble and complain and no one could hear me. And if I looked stupid sitting on that horse, everyone else would be in front of me and couldn't watch me. So off we went, my husband and our three sons smiling and happy with all those other people on the trail. I was not smiling. I was hanging on. It was bumpy and uncomfortable and I knew I was not going to like this. But I would sacrifice my feelings for my family. After all, it was just a simple horse ride and it would be over soon.

The trail leader said I did not have to do much of anything because the horse knew exactly what to do and where to go and would just follow along the trail of the other horses. It would just be a gentle ride through the woods and fields and then back to the horse barn. He also said all I needed to know were two things:

1. Kick my heels in the horse's side to make him go.
2. Pull on the reins to make the horse stop.

"Nothing to worry about." he said. I was hoping the horse heard that.

We started out just fine but as soon as we got into the woods my horse became more and more gentle (and slower and slower). By the time all the other horses were out of the woods, I was still in the woods! I saw our youngest son waving in the distance. I waved back while faking a smile.

This seemed to be the longest ride with just this boring horse and me. Are you supposed to talk to a horse? I didn't know. Besides I certainly did not have anything to say. I didn't even like the horse. However, I did not want to irritate him, because I had heard horses know when you're scared or don't like them, so I would just have to fake him out. We finally got out of the woods and were in a bean field. Suddenly, my horse just stopped. Then I remembered one other important thing the trail leader told me: *"Don't let the horse stop to eat the beans, because then the horse will not want to go back to the barn."* I looked down and the horse was eating the beans. *"Oh my goodness!"* I yelled at the horse, *"Don't eat the beans."* The horse just turned his head and looked at me (I think he was scowling) and kept on eating the beans. Now I would never get back to the barn! What was I supposed to do? Maybe I wasn't nice enough, I thought, so I said to the horse very nicely, *"Please horse. Do not eat the beans."* It didn't matter, because that horse was determined to stay there. I heard the echo of our youngest son yelling at my husband *"Where's mom?"* They all looked back at me, but just kept riding back to the barn. I saw the trail leader motioning with his hand for me to come ahead. *"Let's see,"* I mumbled, *"In order to make the horse go you kick the horse on the sides with your heels."* So, I did and the horse did not move. What's more, I don't think he liked it. He turned his head and looked at me (with one big eye on the side of his head looking straight into mine) and then he nudged my toe with his mouth. I thought he might bite my foot so I took my foot out of the stirrup. *"I'll fool him."* I thought. Kicking did not work! So I tried *"giddy-up."* Giddy-up did not work. So I just said *"GO."* GO was not working either and he just kept right on eating those beans. I wanted to cry, but I figured that wouldn't work either so I just got mad. I said *"Giddy-up"* and *"GO"* louder and louder as I scowled back at the horse. Nothing worked! He was at a dead stop and nothing was going to budge him. Finally, the trail leader must have realized I was in trouble, because he left everyone back at the barn (yes, they were already at the barn) and came back to rescue me, thank heaven. I saw this, but so did the horse. And the horse suddenly got the message that he was in trouble. So, this horse made the decision it was in his best interest to immediately stop eating the beans and get back to that barn as fast as he could. I didn't have to kick. I didn't even have to say *"Giddy-up"* or *"Go"* because he just started to gallop! And he galloped faster and faster in a straight bee-line for the barn!

  Here I was, with only one foot in the stirrups, not much to hang onto and bouncing up and down on this gentle horse who had turned into a galloping fool. I figured if there was a tree branch handy I could always try to grab it and swing right off the horse letting the horse ride off into the sunset without me. After all, it worked in those western movies. I quickly decided it was not a smart idea. Besides, there were no trees in the bean field. The horse and I passed up the trail leader, passed up the entire trail group and went galloping right into the barn door and came to a dead stop. Both of us were out of breath! I must have looked pale, shaken and mad because my husband and three sons rushed to help me get off. They tried not to laugh. My only words were: *"Don't you ever - I repeat, ever ask me to ride any horse again in my entire life!"* They were silent. I was not in any mood to be reckoned with. I think this time they paid attention.

That horse ride was the ride of my life. It was an experience I do not wish to repeat. Yet it sort of imitated our journey of life and faith and the questions that seem to line that journey like tree branches hanging over us.

> How will I hang on?
> What if I fall, or fail?
> What am I doing here?
> What if I look stupid?
> What if I need help?
> What if I make the wrong decision or take the wrong direction?

Keeping the faith sometimes scares me, because maybe I will not do very well. At times I need others to help me take the right trail to the right destination. I want protection around me so I do not have to fall or get hurt. Sometimes there seems to be very little to hang onto. I may want to fake it and make it look like I am doing OK when I am really scared, angry or hurt. I always want to have the gentle ride with the ever constant sunshine through the beautiful woods and the rolling green fields of life. In reality, my ride of life and faith is bumpy and uncomfortable, and at times either too slow, or comes to a dead stop or seems to gallop beyond my control. I may feel alone and lost in a distant field. I would like the power to kick in my heels and say *"Giddy-up"* and pull on the reins and say *"Whoa."* I do not want to 'ride out ' questions and doubts, hurts and problems or hard tasks.

***

We need to realize we do not ride alone and we can eventually stay on the trail and be home with our Lord. If we take a good look around us we will see God riding back to us and helping guide us to where we need to be. He is the Master Guide. He allows us to take the ride even with our wrong decisions, fears, doubts and faithless moments. Yet He is always leading, guiding, surrounding us with his ever present spirit of love no matter which earthly direction we choose to take. And if we can manage to keep and hang onto our faith against all odds, then we can truly have the "ride of our life."

Chapter 3

One by One

At age 15 I wanted a job very badly, but I was not quite old enough to work in a regular business. I found an ad in the newspaper for a "student wanted to take care of children" in someone's home, after school and on Saturdays. Even though I did not have much experience baby-sitting, I thought I would apply anyway. (In fact, the few times I did baby-sit, I didn't know how to handle babies, so I mostly just sat and wished the parents would come home as soon as possible.) The job involved some housework. (My mother couldn't even get me to clean my own room!) I called the woman who placed the ad, and she said I should come to meet and talk with her. I walked there since it was about a mile down the road from our house, in a much nicer neighborhood than my own. The houses there even had dishwashers and televisions.

This job meant going there after school was out, watching the children, sometimes cooking the kids a simple supper if the parents were going out and doing some housecleaning such as sweeping, dusting, vacuuming, scrubbing floors and doing dishes. To my delight, it also included going with the family on their summer vacation for 3 weeks at their lake home. As I sat and talked with the mother I noticed she obviously was pregnant and very excited and happy about it. I surmised she probably wanted help because she was having a second child. While we were talking, in came a little red-headed boy with a truck.

"*Say hi, Jimmy,*" the mother said.
Jimmy said *"Hi!"*

Not knowing much what to say, I said *"hi"* too, and I also asked, *"How old are you?"*

"Six," he answered and he ran out the door. We continued talking and then another little boy came in the door.

"Say hi, Jack," the mother said.

Jack said, *"Hi!"*

Again I said *"Hi."* and *"How old are you?"*

"Five," he answered and out the door he ran. We continued talking.

In came another one, Julie.

I was getting a lump in my throat.

We said *"Hi."* She was four.

We talked. I started to perspire.

Another one came in.

Jeannie. Two and a half.

We kept talking (only I was not listening very well). I was trying to figure out if it was really possible to have this many children under 6 and how this woman could possibly be so happy about being pregnant! Then I heard the sound of a crying child coming from the bedroom. I started to count in my mind. This would be child number 5. Five children and a sixth on the way? How badly did I want this job?

The mother and I went into the bedroom together and there was little Johnny waking up from his nap. He was 15 months old. He smiled at me, AND THAT SMILE DID IT. I somehow just could not resist his smile and cute face with tousled blond hair, beautiful dark eyes and drool flowing down his chin. I took the job. Imagine the shock on my mother's face when I came home and announced I had a job and was going to clean, sweep, dust, vacuum, wash dishes, cook and take care of five children under the age of 6, whose names all started with J. And I was going on a three week summer vacation to a lake home. She must have thought God himself had spoken to me.

After taking the job I wondered how I was going to handle it. It seemed quite overwhelming. I decided to just look at it differently. I was not going to think of it as taking care of five children. I was going to think of it as taking care of them one by one.

I would take care of Jimmy.

Then I would take care of Jack.
Then I would take care of Julie.
Then I would take care of Jeannie.
Then I would take care of Johnny.
ONE BY ONE, it would be workable.

This was not a profound thought. It was a survival tactic (and the lake vacation didn't hurt, either). Anyway, I had the job and it was wonderful. I learned a lot from both the parents and the children. And this "ONE BY ONE" philosophy has stuck with me.

***

I figure a lot of things can be looked at and accomplished ONE BY ONE. Shouldn't we live each day ONE BY ONE? Shouldn't we accept each other, with our failures and our successes ONE BY ONE? Shouldn't we take a look at our problems and try to solve them ONE BY ONE? Isn't it important to have faith and give ourselves to God ONE BY ONE? It's not simple or easy because we tend to look at the large, exaggerated, overextended, overwhelming picture. And it scares us, saddens us, knocks us down and seems to tell us we will not make it. Things can be solved ONE BY ONE. One of the best-known common philosophies is living ONE day at a time. ONE person can do extraordinary things such as - Mother Theresa, Martin Luther King, Mahatma Gandhi and many others in history. I always carry with me the following quote from Edward Everett Hale because it says it all:

I am only one,

But still I am one.

I cannot do everything,

But still I can do something.

And because I cannot do everything,

I will not refuse to do the something that I can do.

And then there is our one Lord, one Savior, one God who is present always. He especially looks at us as individuals. Most likely, when He sees what trouble we humans can get into, He has to have extreme patience with us all ONE BY ONE!

Chapter 4

Surprise, Surprise

Several years ago I bought my second home computer. When I was looking at the files on the old one, I happened across an old term paper apparently one of our sons had written for a college composition course. The topic was our Easter church service. As I read it, I was impressed. It was very well written with beautiful descriptive phrases and deep reflective thoughts beyond what I would expect from a first year college student. Well, I knew exactly which son had written this and I was proud. It was the firstborn son of course. The studious one. The one who never stayed out late on Saturday nights. The one who I never had to wake up to go to church on Sundays. The one who almost went into the priesthood. So I decided I should print that term paper out and send it to him, so he could keep it for posterity. And I did.

About a week later, I got a phone call. Not from the son I had sent the paper to, but from his youngest brother. *"MOM,"* he said rather irritated, *"I wrote that paper on the Easter Service in our Church. How come you sent it to him?"* I tried to remain calm instead of astonished, as I replied, *"You wrote that paper?"* This was the son who seemed to treat church as if it was a social event and who never seemed much interested in whether he went to church or not. He was more into soccer than Sunday School. Yes, he had indeed written that paper for a freshman English class at college and those beautiful words about what his church meant to him.

Surprise, Surprise!

One year our sons and their wives decided they would draw names among themselves for Christmas instead of trying to buy a gift for each person on their limited budgets. I overheard one of the wives asking our second son what kind music CDs he would like. *"Well,"* he said, *"I'm into cello music?"* Into cello music? (My brain was stunned!) This was the son who in college had formed a rock band down in the basement which sent us all running to the top floor of the house closing every door and window on the way. This was the son who in high school walked around with his electric guitar permanently attached to his body. This was the son who thought orchestral or classical music were foreign words.

Again, Surprise, Surprise!

A few years ago, someone from our Church remarked they had been in church in the same state where our oldest son lived and had heard him chanting during the service. They said he had a beautiful voice. *"Our son?"* I asked. *"Are you sure? What was his name? What did he look like?"* They gave me the right name and description. Surely this was a case of mistaken identity. This was the son who could not, would not and should not sing (although I was a good mother and never told him this.) He was not even musical. He tried several instruments and ended up playing a snare drum because it was not necessary to play actual notes. He hated the third grade because he had to learn to play the recorder. He even forgot it at home on purpose so he could get out of music class and threatened to break it into tiny pieces when music class was done for the year. I remember sitting with him and hopelessly trying to teach him how to sing *"Whoopee Ti- Yi- Yo Get Along Little Dogies"* because he was going to be a camp counselor! He actually sang in front of people in church? I don't think so.

A few months later we visited him and his family and went to church. He went straight up to the front of the church and chanted in a beautiful voice. Our son. The non-musical one.

Surprise, Surprise!

***

Life hands us many surprises; not all good ones and not all bad ones. We think we cannot take any more of a difficulty. Surprise, surprise! We do with God's help. We think we will not be able to resolve a situation. Surprise, surprise! We will with God's wisdom. We think we will surely fall apart from the stress and strain. Surprise, surprise! We do not with God's strength. We think that we are all alone forever. Surprise, surprise! We are not. We think that we are not destined for eternal life. Surprise, surprise! We are with God's direction. We are given that wonderful, ever-present, free and generous, right-in-front-of-our-nose surprise. We do not have to search, wait or ask for God's love. It is freely given to us. What a wonderful, beautiful surprise!

Chapter 5

The Disappearing Fence

Our house used to have one of those white wooden fences around the yard. I really never liked it. It was old, and I knew it would need a lot of painting. It didn't even keep anything out or in (like animals or small children). The grass would grow wild and tall beside every fence post and the weed eater always got a workout. I put up with it through a painting or two, but then mentioned to my husband maybe we should consider getting rid of it. He only said *"I like that fence,"* which meant getting rid of this fence was going to be a challenge. One day I sort of pushed a little on one of the fence posts. It moved easily. The wood was starting to rot and was very unstable. Maybe just this one section of the fence could go. It was only an 8-foot section on the driveway side which jutted back toward the house. So I went out with my hammer and knocked down this somewhat small, insignificant section. And then, of course, I had to knock down the section on the other side of the driveway (to make it look even). And so it happened that part of the fence disappeared!

    I never thought of it at the time, but the neighbors probably thought a lady lunatic had moved into the neighborhood. Several months later I was hosting our church youth group. One of our sons and I were sitting outside waiting for the kids to arrive when around the corner came a car bringing one of the boys. His sister was driving. As she attempted to turn into the driveway, she neglected to turn wide enough and hit the corner of the fence, sending two more sections tumbling to the ground. She was absolutely mortified! I, on the other hand, thought it was quite a beautiful sight. She apologized profusely, said she was just learning to drive and begged my forgiveness. I absolutely guaranteed her she was forgiven. (I used my better judgment and decided not to thank her.) Of course, I had to go to the other side of the yard with my hammer to make it even. And so it happened that another part of the fence disappeared! I hid the pile of long planks of fence wood in the bushes next to the house and put the rotten fence posts into the garbage cans. Then I got a brilliant idea. I could use the wooden planks which were not rotten to make a sandbox. So I retrieved the boards, got my handy-dandy saw and started to saw these into smaller lengths. I then spied my husband coming around the corner, home early from work. Up to this point, parts of the fence had disappeared so discreetly that he had not really noticed. I hoped (but it was not very likely) he would go directly into the house. Not a chance! He headed straight for me, looking very curious.

"What are you doing?" he asked. "I am making a nice, big, sturdy wonderful sandbox for our children to play in." I answered.

"Can I do anything to help?" he kindly asked.

"Well," I whined, "would you mind sawing this last board? It's very tough wood." (I was entering dangerous territory now.)

"Sure," he said. He sawed quickly through that board while I hoped the wood did not look vaguely familiar.

And so from those broken-down pieces of fence wood we had a nice, big, white ("sturdy as a fence") sandbox. It seemed like sort of a monument to the old fence and would be used for years to come, I thought gallantly.

It was now the next year and part of the old fence still remained. Then one day I decided to mention to my husband how old and rotten this fence which was getting. So rotten that the children might get a lot of large, dangerous slivers. He relented and guessed it better be taken down. So then I, our sons and a few of their friends with hammers in hand, had a great 'knock down the fence day.' And so it happened that the last of the old fence disappeared. And finally one day the part of the fence which was lingering around my garden was replaced by something new and shiny. CHAIN LINK! It was exciting. It was like a new era and a new beginning. In the next few years we had put chain link around our back yard and a dog kennel. Finally, I felt I had settled with that old fence.

And so it can happen that we too, in life, can break down fences and settle old issues such as:

Between us and the family member who we have not spoken to in many years;

Between us and the friend that we felt really hurt us;

Between people who have a different lifestyle which we do not agree with;

Between persons who do not have the same skin color as us;

Between persons who do not speak the same language we do;

Between us and the very God whom we are angry with because of the problems we must endure.

***

We can knock down fences all at once or a little at a time. Our faith can be our hammer. Strong and firm. Molded and shaped with God's love and presence. And when we knock down those fences we can replace them with something shiny and new. A new era and a new beginning. Then we can feel as if we have settled with those old fences. It's never too late with God.

Chapter 6

Midwestern Sharks

I was approached one summer by our 12-year-old son and his best friend. They wanted me to drive them to a nearby town to hunt for sharks teeth. *"Sharks' teeth?"* I said. *"Why on earth would you find sharks' teeth here in the Midwest? There aren't any oceans here!"*

"But," the boys informed me *"there used to be a million years ago and this old guy* (40 or 50 *years old they said) told us that if you go in this certain creek you can find all these prehistoric sharks' teeth."*

"Yeah, right," I said. *"And you believed him? Sharks in the Midwest?"*

Well, they begged and they knew the word pre-historic would get to me. I was overcome by my curiosity.

"OK, this Saturday we'll drive there in search of sharks teeth," I said rolling my eyes. Then I made a secret phone call to my own "old guy" connection whom I knew would know the real story. I asked him if that could possibly be true. Surprisingly he told me the boys were right.

So these two boys started making ready to hunt for sharks' teeth in the Midwest, of all places! They worked very hard getting ready for the hunt, as I looked on in amazement, but mostly in confusion. First of all they needed large shovels. So they gathered all the shovels in both households.

"Oh, what the heck!" I thought and placed my own little garden shovel in the pile, too. Then they needed some old wooden Coca-Cola cases with handles.

"What are those for?" I asked.

"*A sluice box of course,*" they answered.
"*Well, silly me,*" I said. "*What's a sluice box?*"
They explained they were going to make their own sluice box by removing the bottom of the box and replacing it with wire screening so we could shovel the mud into the box, then rinse the mud with water because that is how to find sharks' teeth. Shovel the mud? Rinse the mud? My, how much fun this was going to be! We then visited several neighbors, friends, acquaintances, garage sales, Goodwill stores and even the Coca-Cola company to get the pop cases. And the boys worked hard to make several of those funny sluice boxes.
"*Do I get one too?*" I muttered sheepishly. (In case there was going to be something to this, I didn't want to be left out.) Next they needed lots of small plastic containers or jars with lids to hold all the hundreds of sharks' teeth that we were going to find. Just to go along with their optimism, I contributed several of these and also stuck a couple in my own pocket.
"*Don't forget the boots!*" The boys reminded me.
"*Boots?*" I asked.
"*Of course,*" they said, "*for wading in the water.*" They looked at me with a look which told me they knew I did not get it. Wading in the water? Shoveling and rinsing mud? This was getting quite complicated.
Saturday morning came and we began to load the shark teeth hunting equipment into our Chevrolet Suburban. Thank heaven we had a car that big. The shovels were loaded, the plastic tubes were in our pockets, those red-and-white Coca-Cola sluice boxes were piled behind the seats and two 12-year-old boys, this mother and three little brothers who either begged or were forced to come along so they wouldn't be home alone, climbed into the car, ready to experience shark teeth hunting in the Midwest. Off we drove with directions to some distant creek scribbled on a small piece of paper. The bad news is that a wind came along and the paper flew out the window on the freeway. The boys weren't worried because they just knew we could find it without directions! Nearing the town now, the boys had a sense it was probably down this gravel road which looked like it went nowhere. They were right! It went nowhere! After driving down the road and around the bend we ended up at a cow pasture.
"*This a cow pasture.*" I said.

I Thought There Was a Road There

The boys were all excited! What I saw was a pasture of grazing cows. What they saw was the old creek! And they were having visions of sharks' teeth. Once I stopped staring at the cows, I saw the creek, too. We were there. It did exist! We all put on our boots, flew out of the car past the cows, squeezed ourselves through the barbed wire fence and nearly fell straight down to the creek bank and into the water, shovels and sluice boxes in hand. The hunt was about to begin! And hunt we did. We waded in our boots, shoveled and dug into that muddy, murky water and slung that mud into our Coca-Cola sluice boxes. We rinsed that mud with a vengeance while the cows looked on mooing at us. I cannot forget the moment when I actually found my first shark tooth! It was nearly a spiritual experience! We all found sharks' teeth right there in the mud. Right there where they were supposed to be. Right there where they were a million years ago! What excitement! And when the little brothers started to whine and complain about being tired and the big brothers were satisfied, having found hundreds of sharks' teeth, this mother, covered with dirt, was still digging and shoveling and rinsing the mud to find more sharks' teeth. Something I never thought I would look upon as a kind of treasure! When we finally reached home laughing and all excited, we spread those sharks' teeth out on the dining room table. Then proudly told everyone and anyone who would listen that there really used to be sharks in the Midwest. Some are still not believers, but we are. We were there. What a remarkable experience. I'm glad I didn't miss it.

***

Life itself has doubts and unclear directions and no detailed map. It is very easy to think we're going nowhere. However, we have something special. We have our own 'old guy' connection. It is God and He is an eternal connection. We may have doubts along our journey and the path may not always be evident. We may not always have a detailed map and may not think we are going anywhere. What we may see is a pasture full of problems and hurts. What God sees is a place for each one of us by His side in eternal salvation. Like the sharks' teeth were around millions of years ago and still can be found today, God's love for us was present then and still can be found today. God gives us the equipment we need to dig, shovel and rinse the things of this life. We just need to be wise enough to use it. I figure God puts on his boots, gets right down with us and wades in that muddy, murky water. Then He shovels with us through the soil and grime of life. He rinses us with His blessings, forgiveness and love. He is right there in life with us. He is right there where He is supposed to be. He is right there where He has always been. Faith, like a gigantic sluice box, allows us to rinse away the soiled nature of human failings and find treasures in ourselves and others. We do not have to go it alone. We can dig through life together with God beside us. We can tell people that there really was and still is a loving God. What a remarkable experience. We can be glad we are not missing it!

Chapter 7

The Homeless Man and the Brainless Woman

I've been in a few cities where there are a good number of homeless people. This bothers me. I'm never quite sure exactly what I can do about it except to do my small part of helping at the local soup kitchen when I can or contributing food to the city food pantry. However, there is one sight which really bothers me a lot! It's when I see a man standing on a street corner holding a sign on which is scribbled, **"Homeless. Will work for food."**

It's really difficult for me to look into that man's eyes. I admire him for having the courage to stand there announcing to the world he is homeless and does not even have food to eat.

Some may find it easy to think he is not really homeless, but just lazy or panhandling instead. I don't think that's for me to judge. Instead I just look, drive by and let it bother me.

One day as I drove to the grocery store I saw a man standing on the corner with a crude handmade sign saying exactly that...**"Homeless. Will work for food."** Yes, it bothered me! So as I drove by (being bothered) a voice in my head saying, "If it bothers you so much why don't you do something about it? Put your money where your mouth is! After all, you're going to the grocery store to get all kinds of groceries for yourself and your own family so why not get something for him?" I listened to the voice and then told myself I was absolutely right!

So I went into the grocery store and decided as I went through the aisles picking up my own groceries, I would also try to pick out food for the homeless man. Then I changed my plan. What I really needed to do,

I thought, was get his food first, since he may start walking somewhere. Yes, I would get his food first.

First of all, I should get him some kind of sandwich and so I debated as to what kind of sandwich I would get. Beef or ham? (But what if he was a vegetarian?) Tuna or chicken salad? (Some vegetarians don't eat fish or chicken either. Besides it might have mayonnaise on it and that could spoil. I certainly couldn't tell him he had to eat it right away so it wouldn't spoil.) Peanut butter and jelly? That would be perfect but the store didn't make those. What was I to do? I finally decided on a big deli sandwich with all different meats and cheeses. A 'man's' sandwich! That would fill him up. I was really thinking!

Next, I needed to get something to go with the sandwich. Potato chips? (Of course they might get crushed if he put them in his pocket while he was hitchhiking. Who likes crushed chips?) Popcorn? (Popcorn with a sandwich didn't seem quite right.) Fruit? (It might spoil and I didn't know which fruit he liked.) Ah, so many decisions! I finally got a whole box of potato chips because they came in a more sturdy canister so they would be protected. Oh, clever me!

Now a dessert. Ice cream would melt. Candy was not too healthy. Cream pie might spoil. Cookies might be OK, but might crumble. Cake might get crushed and the frosting was messy. Maybe he would be too full from all this food I was getting, so he would need a dessert that would keep well and not fall apart. Finally, I settled on a Rice Krispy bar. I was on a roll now!

Then something to drink! Now here was a challenge. Milk? (What it he didn't like milk? Besides it might spoil.) Pop? (People I know are so fussy about what kind of pop they like to drink and pop has a lot of sugar in it and that's not healthy.) Fruit juice? (Juice is terrifically healthy, but what kind?) This was getting to be difficult deliberation. Then it came to me. Mineral water! It was healthy, would not spoil, could be recapped and could be carried easily. I was brilliant! I got him a name brand fancy mineral water. In fact, I got him two bottles. I was proud of myself! Finally, my task was complete. Then more questions crept into my mind. Questions in my mind like, Did I really get healthy food? Since it was almost suppertime did I really buy things that were more for lunch? What if it wasn't enough for him or too much and he'd have to throw it out because he had no place to put it? What if he hated everything I got? What if he had a terrible allergic reaction to something that I bought and had to go to the hospital and then I would feel terrible. (Did I really think I was going to hang around to watch him eat and see what happens?) Then more questions came into my mind. What if he got angry because I only brought him food and did not have any work for him? Should I get out of the car or hand it to him through the window? I didn't want to act scared or not good enough to approach him. What if I got so emotional I started to cry and he thought I was strange? Then as I looked at my watch, I asked my last question. What if he's gone by now? I rushed to the checkout, paid for the food, leaped into my car and drove to the end of the block to give the food to him and he was gone! *'How dare he move,* I thought. Now what was I supposed to do? I was trying to do a good deed here. Suddenly I felt terribly foolish. Of course it was my own fault for not just getting to the task, buying the food and taking it out right away. I drove around several blocks hunting for this homeless stranger. I was determined to do my good deed. Then, all of a sudden I spotted him standing on a different corner. I pulled right up to him, got out of the car and handed him the food. He took the food, smiled and simply said, *"Bless you."*

    I'm sure he didn't know what a long exhausting process I had just gone through and I was not about to tell him. He would probably think I was surely in need of mental help. Then I drove away and nothing extraordinary happened. As I got out into the main street and was waiting for the light to turn green, I looked over at him. He was examining those fancy brand name bottles of mineral water with a puzzled look. Then he opened the sandwich, placed the canister of chips beside him and stuck the Rice Krispy bar in his pocket.

    It was so simple. He needed food. I could give the food. But I had to make this giving of food into a big production and ask myself too many questions. And make a simple thing into a complicated process while nearly missing my chance to do the right thing. I should have been standing on the corner with a sign of my own saying…**"Need Common Sense."**

    This experience reminds me sometimes we do this same thing with our lives. We let things bother us as we 'drive by' but don't do anything about them. When things could be simple, we tend to make them complicated. We ask too many questions we could not possibly have or even need the answers to. We run around in circles instead of getting to the task with graciousness and humility. We don't just get out of the car and give the food and help each other with no questions, no extensive contemplating and no judgment. How many of us have the courage of that homeless man on the corner?

***

In God's eyes we are no different than that homeless man. We are both equally accepted by God. God does not spend time wondering about us and asking a million questions. He just accepts us. We do not have to stand on the corner with a sign that says "Faithless - Need Spiritual Food." God just "gets out of the car" so to speak and gives us our spiritual food. It is that simple. No questions asked, no extensive contemplating, no judgment and no complex process. He expects very little. He only asks that we have faith. God takes our faith, smiles on us and says very simply... *"Bless you."*

Chapter 8

When I Lost the Need to Know

I can nearly remember the exact moment several years ago when I began to lose credibility with my children. When they turned into teenagers, I started having difficulty functioning while they were in the same room. Once when we were on vacation and in a hotel room, I refused to try to set the digital clock. Of course my teenagers, never having seen this particular clock before, seemed to be able to work every button. The hotel drapes should have been fairly simple to manage, but I couldn't even get those opened. Instead I almost poked my eye out on some new-fangled plastic rod.

"Just pull that plastic rod, Mom. What's the matter?" asked one of my teenagers. *"Don't you know how to open curtains?"*

"I used to.", I answered.

Why is it that a teenage boy who never owned a microwave can show you how it works 10 seconds after it's out of the box. He can learn a computer so fast it sends your brain spinning! He can hook up all kinds of wires to stereos, lighting systems, guitars and amplifiers without instructions. But ask him to run the weed-eater and he doesn't know how! I ask myself if teenage boys are so good at some things then why can't they..........?

Aim and hit the wastebasket.
Put their clothes in the closet on hangers.
Study without the TV and stereo on.
Use a plate for potato chips and pretzels.

Turn OFF a light switch.
Mow the lawn or shovel the snow without 12 bathroom breaks.
Remember to put gas in their car.
Drink from a glass instead of the milk carton.
Go to the library more than 2 hours before a term paper is due.
Ask to play an inexpensive band instrument.
Turn on a lamp when reading in the dark.
Shave even if they only have 5 (long) hairs on their face.

Leave a note at least every third day as to their whereabouts when you have not seen them awake and upright recently.

Stop saving old candy and gum wrappers in their underwear drawers.

Write legibly.

I had five years of college! I am an educated person! Yet there was that point when my college age sons began to write term papers on psychology, philosophy and micro-organisms which read as if they were from another galaxy. I just didn't get it! Maybe sometimes I look stupid wearing thick socks in my dress shoes to stretch them out. So what! So I don't always pronounce "parmesan" and "pasta" right. So what! Once, only once, did I call the accelerator in the car the "foot feet" (or was it the "foot feed?"). Even my 80-year-old mother couldn't believe I said that. So what if I get confused trying to run the VCR. I can program it to record something 2, 3, or 4 weeks from now, but can't seem to get it to run at this very moment.

I think I am an intelligent person. I work. I run a household. I am very organized. I give professional presentations. I can speak to co-workers in an articulate way. People say I do a good job. I have friends. So what has happened to me?

The truth is that we all know different "stuff" at different times. It's like everything else is based on the need to know. A teenager needs to know about wires and speakers to communicate with his friends. He needs to know about computers in order to "surf the Net" like his peers. These things are important to his present life. He will learn to turn off the lights when he is paying the light bill, he will learn to plan, get information and write a good paper when his paycheck depends on it, he will learn to use the weed eater when it is his own suburban green grass and he will learn to have plenty of gas in the car when he is traveling with his own teenagers.

Back when I was a teenager, it was not yet my time to need to know all about computers and VCRs. (I am getting better at the computer, however, I'm still not so sure about the VCR.) I developed the need to know how to run the VCR because I did not want to miss seeing some of the things my grandchildren were doing. At a former job I was actually forced to have a need to know about using a computer when a secretary quit and all my information was on the computer. Somehow I had to get the information out of there! I have come to the conclusion I will never live long enough to learn everything that even my own computer does. Computers will keep me busy the rest of my functional life. If I had not had that urgent need to know I would not be writing these thoughts now.

When we have that need to know, we will learn and we will pick and choose our "stuff" to know just like the teenager. And there will always be more "stuff" to know. Life is so full of interesting information which we indeed must choose. Then there is plenty of other "stuff" that I don't even want to begin to know. Like the stock market or politics.

***

There is one item on life's agenda which is NOT based on the need to know. And that is to know God and his love. We do not need complicated directions. We do not need a college degree. We actually don't even have to be organized or articulate. We can be in our homes or homeless, we can have skin of any color, we can be poor or rich, we can be happy or sad, we can be old or young. We can even be angry with God. We can accept God's love anytime, anyplace without waiting for a "need to know" urge.

Chapter 9

The Struggle

It was a Friday night and I had just arrived at the wrestling match event. I had not eaten supper, but I really wasn't very hungry. I had some snacks in my purse because I knew I would be hungry later, but not yet. No, not just yet. Lots of people were gathering and taking their seats and chatting. I was very nervous, as I always was on evenings like this. However, I made the most of it because I really wanted to be here. I had my prayer already in my head to say at just the right time.

Then the main attractions came out onto the floor; my oldest son among them. And soon the knot started forming in my stomach. It was fun, but difficult to watch my son being thrown all over the mat, grappling for the top position, turning pale, bleeding from the nose and having the coach stuff wads of cotton up into his nose while telling him to go out there and pin the other guy. Being a nurse did not help matters at all. I thought they should have a better bedside manner as well as just stop the darn match. But, in the wrestling world this was just a minor matter. I remember once taking our son at six in the morning down to the high school bus to travel to a wrestling tournament in another state. He had his arm in a sling, a splint on his finger and one eye bruised and nearly swollen shut. I could not believe I was actually taking him there. However, he assured me he could still wrestle. (I think he even won that day!)

This night's match would probably be much like the other ones, I thought. The knot in my stomach would stay there until he was done wrestling. I would yell only silently inside, because I did not know quite what to say if I yelled and I did not want to yell anything stupid to embarrass our son. I would say my silent prayer just before he stepped onto the mat...

> *"God, Please let him win.*
> *But if that's not possible,*
> *At least don't let him get hurt."*

I know it was a somewhat selfish prayer but it suited me and I had it timed just right for a couple of seconds before he started. And when he was done wrestling my stomach would feel better, I would have a snack out of my purse, signal to him that he did good (even if he did not win) and go home thankful he did not get seriously hurt.

Tonight's match was just starting and he was somewhat evenly matched with his opponent. It was extremely hard to tell who was winning. The match went the full three minutes. Both boys were getting tired and getting nowhere. So they went into overtime for one more long minute of struggling and getting nowhere. They were really tired now and moving pretty slowly. That overtime minute ended and now there would be another minute overtime. Both boys just stared at each other in a daze. Or it could have been utter disbelief that they had to go once again into overtime. They could hardly move towards each other. That next minute seemed to last forever, their skin pale and dripping with perspiration. I was screaming inside thinking they would never make it off the mat because they were so exhausted. I could not believe there would be a third minute of overtime. What kind of inhumane and cruel punishment was this anyway? They looked and moved like they were in slow motion, their faces showing no emotion but they managed to make some attempt at grasping each other's bodies once in a while. I was sure they were just going to collapse in a heap any minute. No human being could or should have to go on like this! (And no mother should have to watch this.)

The final overtime minute ended and they both collapsed in unison with a thud on the mat. The winner would be by decision. Both boys struggled to get onto their feet slowly and weaved with fatigue. Then the decision was announced and our son was declared the winner! What I saw at that moment was unbelievable. Our son suddenly jumped into the air with an explosion of enthusiasm and energy, smiling and exuberant! How he managed this I do not know. But when it came to the definite end, the ultimate decision time, the time that mattered, he was renewed and ecstatic. The picture of him leaping into the air is still imprinted on my memory. I will never forget his suspension in the air, his renewal of energy and the smile on his face. It was an ecstatic moment for both of us.

***

How many of us have struggled, too, with all kinds of issues in our lives. While our loving God, our protector, allows us to struggle on as we look up and wonder why. We grapple on the wrestling mat of life constantly. We go headlong into difficult issues, broken and wondering whether we will survive, much less win. We continue to ask God why and many times not receiving what we would consider good answers. We think we have things solved in good time, then discover that we may also have to go into overtime on the mat of life to struggle over and over, again and again. There are those who cheer for us and those who cheer against us. We say silent prayers to help us along the way. We are not always declared a winner by decision and sometimes the other guy wins. But when we win, I hope each and every one of us can feel like our son did at the end of that match, exuberant and happy and grateful, even if only for a few moments. And I hope we can see fit to thank our God for allowing us to struggle in order to have that ultimate moment in everlasting life when we will step onto the mat of heaven next to God himself, where we need struggle no more.

Chapter 10

To Be or Not To Be...a Sheep

During one Christmas season, our son and daughter-in-law were co-directors of their church's Sunday School. Each Christmas, the Sunday School acted out the story of Jesus' birth. It is quite a production and not an easy task to organize about 30 kids of all ages in learning their lines and roles, as well as distributing and planning a limited number of costumes for each role. The youngest children always have the role of being the sheep. In their fluffy, white woolly hand-made sheep costumes, they get to make a grand entrance ambling down the church aisle on all fours to stand in the stable where Jesus was born. The next oldest children, dressed as angels, walk sweetly down the aisle as their homemade wings swish and the organist plays Christmas carols. Then the next oldest children get to be the shepherds and wise men, wearing make-shift bath robed costumes and towels over their heads. Two of the older ones get to be Mary and Joseph. Older teenagers take turns narrating parts of the Christmas story as the scene is played out in front of the overcrowded church audience, parents' heads stretching and "oohing" and "aahing" over their children's entrances.

Our granddaughter, age four, was assigned to the sheep group. However, this particular year she decided she did not want to be a sheep. She wanted to be an angel or maybe even Mary. No small roles for her. Her mother explained in so many words that she had to be a sheep this year, because she wasn't old enough yet to fit into the angel costumes nor was she old enough to handle Mary's part of the script. And it would not be fair to take away one of the older girls' angel costumes away, because it was their turn to be angels. They had been in the sheep roles when they were her age. However, our granddaughter would not be deterred. If she could not be an angel or Mary she would not be anything. She absolutely refused to be a sheep! Even after an explanation that she would not be able to be in the play with the other children, she would not change her mind. Her mom and dad, Coordinators of the whole Sunday School, had to accept the fact their very own daughter would not be in the play because of her stubbornness.

Sunday morning, on the way to Church, when they were halfway there, our granddaughter announced, *"I guess I want to be a sheep!"* Frustrated, her parents explained she had already fussed and made her decision not to be a sheep and all the sheep costumes had been distributed. The only way she could still be a sheep was if one of the "sheep" kids was not there and she could wear their costume. But it would not be fair to take away someone else's sheep costume now. Our granddaughter frowned and pouted but did not say a word. Then her mother asked her why she had decided to become a sheep now, when she had said before that no way was she going to be a sheep. They got the answer. What had happened was at church the day before, the priest had asked her, *"And are you going to be a little sheep?"* She had sweetly replied, *"Uh-huh."* She had somehow suddenly remembered that she had told the priest she would be a sheep. Luckily, when they arrived at the Church and began to get ready for the program, one of the little boys was sick. Lucky because now she could be a sheep. Her mother helped her into the sheep costume. She should have been happy now, but instead she complained the sheep costume was uncomfortable and not "close enough to her body" as she called it, and it was too fluffy! Her mom explained sheep were supposed to be fluffy. Reluctantly, she did keep the sheep costume on and went along with the rest of the "herd" down the church aisle.

The program went on as planned and immediately after the program when the applause died down, the priest stepped in front of the smiling group of Sunday School children, turned toward our granddaughter and asked her to come and stand by him. Horrified, her parents, each on a different side of the church, looked at each other across the room, not knowing what was going to happen and certain she would either cry or have a tantrum in front of the entire congregation. The priest then proceeded to tell everyone about the struggle with being a sheep. (Her parents must have hinted to the priest that she was having trouble with the sheep role.) He said, "You know, one of the little girls here was not sure she wanted to be a sheep today. But as you see, she is here with the rest of the children. You know, Jesus loves everyone because everyone is important. He loves sheep just as much as everything and everybody else. It does not matter what or who you are. Jesus always loves you. He came down to save each and every one of us, even a sheep." He went on to thank the Sunday school directors and all the children. And as her parents drew a deep breath of relief, there stood our little 4-year-old granddaughter holding onto the old priest's hand, looking up at him with baby blue eyes, smiling with a rather Mona Lisa smile... and being a sheep.

***

I really understand how she felt. Sometimes I don't want to be a sheep either. Most of the time I am satisfied with what I am, but there are some occasions (more rare as I get older) when I don't want to be what I am. I would rather be someone else or somewhere else and doing something else. At times I think life is not fair and if I cannot be what and where I want to be I will be stubborn and not be anything. And I too will refuse to be a sheep, refuse to accept what I really am. Like our granddaughter's too-fluffy sheep costume, things become uncomfortable and they do not really fit right.

But then I find myself, like our granddaughter, reluctantly reverting back to, once again, being a sheep, being what I am. And as I am standing there feeling rather insignificant and unimportant, God seems to beckon me to stand beside Him, takes my hand in His, smiles down on me, gives me his love and peace and understanding for my humanness and lets me know He sent Jesus for me just as much as anyone else and it is perfectly OK to be a sheep.

Chapter 11

The Future is Coming

The following is a school essay written by one of our sons, when he was 13 years old:

"Ten years from now I will be at the University majoring in medical science. I'll be graduating and planning to be a great medical researcher. When I graduate I will go home first and visit my parents. Then I'll go to work at the University Hospital. After I have solved a number of questions about various common and some uncommon diseases, I will take a long vacation and set up my own laboratory in my basement of the medium-sized house I will buy. I might even start my own private medical practice. I will try to find cures to diseases such as cancer, heart disease and even the common cold. Hopefully, I will be successful and have a very smart assistant. I also hope that I will have written many books and articles about the science of medicine. With the $100,000.00 I will make, I will buy a fancy car with an exterior of white wall tires, tinted glass, chrome plated accessories and a fine engine. The car will have an interior of velvet covered front and back seats, a real leather dashboard, an AM-FM stereo tape player, speakers in front and back, a built-in bar and television set, and of a course, a telephone. And last, but not least, a shofer. (he needed to learn to spell better). One of the trips I would like to make will be for my research; a trip to Africa to investigate the disease called sleeping sickness which is caused by the tsetse bug. The other pleasure trips I would like to make are to Paris, because I think it would be exciting to see the Eiffel tower for the first time, and I would also like to visit Greece and see where my father grew up. After that I would just take life as it is."

Now, let me suppose what I would have written when I was 13 years old:

"Ten years from now I probably will not go to college but will become the secretary to the President of the United States, who will always be a Democrat of course. I will never go into the health field because sick people make me sick. (I went into Nursing.) I will get married to someone with a less complicated Norwegian last name than mine. Someone with a short, simple last name. (My married name is 14 letters long and Greek.) I will be a housewife as well as a very popular singer and dancer on the side. I will make several musical movies with famous singers and dancers and make a fortune from these and live in Hollywood, where I will actually own a TV set and be able to afford to buy Tupperware. In my spare time I will write great poetry that will be read throughout the entire world. I will have 6 children (3 boys and 3 girls) and they will be perfect and never talk back to me and agree with everything I say because I will be the perfect parent. I will get a great amount of exercise every day and will be thin all my life. I will vacation in the jungles of Africa where there is no winter and no snow. After that I will take life as it is."

Taking life as it is. That's the hard part. Because it is never how we happen to see life at age 13. After all the 13-year-old dreaming of being a medical scientist, our son now is a band teacher. And a good one and that's where he belongs. He knew this when he learned to play his first instrument, a saxophone. He knew this when he received the Louis Armstrong Award in high school. He knew this when he developed a passion for jazz. He knew this when he enrolled in a School of Music at a university. His life is far from medical discoveries, far from $100,000 and far from fancy cars with chauffeurs. However, he has musical discoveries, a steady income and a Ford. And he does take life as it is and he is happy. That is what's really important. I, on the other hand, never got to be a secretary to the President (I had to take typing twice), I am not thin, my last name is not simple and I cannot sing. Instead of great poetry, I am writing nursing material about bedpans and stomach tubes. I have not been the perfect parent and neither are my children perfect, but all of us have tried our best to do the right and decent things. My children still call, speak to me and like to come home once in a while.

We have three televisions and I have an entire drawer overflowing with Tupperware. What more could a woman ask for? I have never been in the jungles of Africa and I live in the winter of the Midwest. More than half of my life has been spent at the bedside of sick people. They do not make me sick. Instead I have thousands of images of the sick embedded in my memory and not one regret about this. I am grateful that I could have some small part in their healing and in some cases in their passing from this earth. They were my real teachers of how to care for the sick and they taught me well. At my nursing graduation, the speaker, who was a minister, said to all of us, *"Remember that you may be the last person that patient sees, the last voice that patient hears, and the last person that patient touches."* I knew right then and there that I was not meant to become a secretary, or a singer and dancer or go live in the jungles of Africa. I knew I was where I should be.

***

I think all that God asks us to do is to accept where we are at this moment, on this day, at this time and at this place. And accept what we are and what others are. After all, He accepts us as we are whether or not we are making wonderful scientific discoveries or becoming famous and whether we see ourselves as successful or not.

A priest once gave a wonderful sermon on what success really is. He asked, *"Is it money? Is it fame? Is it expensive cars or other material things? Is it a very important high class job? Is it all kinds of good deeds?"* His answer was very simple. "To God success is faith and faith alone. That is all we need and it is all that God expects from us." After that, as our son stated so simply, we can "take life as it is."

Chapter 12

Stuck Where I Did Not Belong

One day when I was pregnant with our first child, I went shopping at a large department store downtown. Eager to buy my first maternity outfit, since I was not fitting very well into anything else anymore, I headed straight for the maternity department. I wasn't exactly very big yet, just big enough not to fit in regular clothes. I began trying on maternity clothes, which in those years were always two-piece. (Funny no one had yet figured out how ugly they were and that it would be much better to make one-piece outfits.) I tried on several outfits in the "fitting" room, then went out to the three-way mirror to see how each one looked. What a sight! Not pregnant enough to show, but desperate enough to need to buy something. I looked like someone who could not tell what size to buy. The outfits were like tents and swished around my body like waves of cloth not quite sure where to go.

During one trip, as I attempted to retreat back to the fitting room, I was met by several young women in three-inch heels going the opposite direction. I tried to fight my way back to the fitting room, but for some reason they were in a very big hurry and being much taller, paid no attention to me. (I thought I was tall at five feet and five inches, but these woman seemed to be at least six feet tall since I remember looking straight into jewelry, furs and fancy dresses instead of seeing any faces.) I also remember smelling lots of perfume. They just kept on coming and I was forced to join them going in the opposite direction out some kind of exit into the middle of a circle shaped area. When the bright spotlights hit me in the face, I realized that I had been mobbed by a bunch of department store models into a fashion show area. And there I was in those awful maternity clothes staring straight into the crowd under a spotlight! Mortified? Yes! Almost to the point of nausea. Thank heaven that did not happen.

You have never seen a pregnant woman exit so fast back to the fitting room, where I stayed for a very long time, until I was certain that the fashion show was over, not wanting to show my face or my pregnant body again.

***

I think sometimes that happens to all of us. We get pushed and shoved where we really do not belong. Stuck in the wrong line or in the wrong situation. Following the crowd, going in the opposite direction that we want to. Others looming tall over us and carrying us right along with them into an unknown situation. Stuck at a distance from God. Wondering if He has abandoned us and why. Thinking that His word and promise doesn't seem to fit at the moment. And when we actually see where we are headed and realize what is happening, we have to struggle and push and shove our way back to where we really belong. And maybe even hide out until things blow over. It can be done no matter how mortified or ugly we feel. We can always sneak back and wait until we can emerge safely once again. But we need a lot of help from God. And He is always there beside us, willing and able to help us with the correct "fit", the correct direction and the correct path to Faith.

Chapter 13

My Mother, God, and President Truman

When my mother turned 86 years old, I had to move her to the same town where I lived. The 10 months which followed were extremely stressful for me. Only then and I mean only then, did I really understand what others of the "sandwich generation" had known all along about the stress of placing your parent into a nursing home. Never mind that I am a nurse. It was different! It was my mother! Shortly after moving, she had five medical procedures and two major surgeries in a timespan of six months. Then in the fall, when my husband and I were vacationing in the mountains of Greece, she had an emergency admission to the hospital and had to be moved into a nursing home. My ordeal of faith then really began! (I am tempted to call it a nightmare, but I don't think God would like that.)

The Mother Part

Even though my mother and I had discussed she probably would have to go into a nursing home, even though I had started the piles and piles of complicated paperwork and forms, neither of us were ready for this. We both knew this was what had to be, but we were both angry. She knew she had to be there, but hated it. I knew she had to be there and also hated it. We were in for quite an experience!

The mother I placed in the nursing home was really not at all like my mother, at least not the mother I had known in the past. Not the laughing, understanding, kind to everyone, encouraging, "this too shall pass" tough person that I had known all my life. She always had an encouraging and kind word for everyone. She was always polite and appreciative of anything anyone did for her. She always helped and gave to others even though she had very little herself. Now she was somebody else who I hardly knew. Someone who behaved differently now. However, I felt I was still the same person. I was a nurse who was kind and understanding, patient and yet tough. I knew all about health care. However before long, I too, turned into someone else. Someone I did not recognize as me. Let me give you some examples,

One day I visited my mother and she announced, *"The Avon lady came!"*

I replied, *"Oh no, Mother, the Avon lady does not come here. You are thinking of when you* were *in your apartment. You are mistaken."*

My mother said, *"No, the Avon lady did come here and I ordered some face cream!"*

So I said. *"Sure, Mother."* I smiled and knew (because I was a qualified health-care professional) she probably was just confused.

Three days later I again went to visit her and there on the bedside table were two jars of Avon face cream. She saw the shocked look on my face and smugly said, *"I told you that the Avon lady came!"*

Another day my mother told me she was not getting her mail. It was going to her roommate. *"Oh, Mother,"* I said, *"You probably just thought your roommate got it. Your name is on the door, everyone knows who you are. Don't worry, you will always get your mail!"*

A week later the Social Worker called me to tell me someone had put the names on the door in the wrong order and also there was a new volunteer delivering the mail. My mother had not been getting her mail.

This time when I visited my mother she told me, *"They changed the sign on the door. They got me and my roommate mixed up. I was not getting my mail!"* This time I only said, *"Yes, Mother."*

It was a time when I frantically wanted everything to go perfectly without any stress and without any problems. I argued with her, I rarely took her words seriously and I acted as if I was her mother. During the next few months she told me several times, *"You are getting pretty smart-alecky!"* Well, things did not get much better. She was miserable. I was miserable. She hated the situation and so did I. She fought everything, and I tried to fix everything. The situation seemed hopeless. Her condition got worse; she became anemic from some internal bleeding and her one and only functioning kidney was not very good. Her thyroid function was low, she had back pain and she could not manage her own hearing aids. She refused to read, write or call anyone and would not go to any function including church services at the nursing home, even though she had always been a faithful churchgoer. She did not like anything or anybody. Then one week she became very confused and had to be once again admitted into the hospital, where it was discovered that she had had two small strokes.

The God Part

Yes, this is where God comes in. Now, I was going to deal with God. This was not fair! Why did my mother have to be like this? Why was getting old so miserable? Why do people have to be old and sick? Why was this so difficult? How long is this going to go on? And what on earth was the darn purpose to all this*? "Well",* I answered myself, *"there was no purpose! My mother was right."* (This was the only thing we agreed on at the time, that there was no purpose to all of this.) After being in the hospital a week my mother returned to the nursing home after what seemed to be like a "tune-up" in the hospital. She received blood, iron medication, a change in other medications, some fluid control and physical therapy. I wanted to say to God. *"Well, God, what now? Back to where she is still miserable and still feels useless with no purpose? Tell me, God! What now?"*

I think at that very moment God looked down at my mother and said, *"She really is pretty smart-alecky, isn't she?"* Then things changed. My mother actually said she was "almost" (I repeat "almost") glad to be back in the nursing home. Little by little she began to learn to use her wheelchair, going in to watch the bird aviary, calling some of the staff by name and knowing which ones she liked the best. She even teased and laughed out loud with some of them. One day she gave me a list of books she wanted to read. She started attending church services and going to some of the activities. One day she even asked me to bring her cards and stamps so she could write some letters.

***

I suddenly realized what God had in mind for me. He was telling me there was hope. He was telling me that I was a good health professional with other mothers, but not so good with my own. He was telling me not to be so smart-alecky! And He was absolutely right. After that I learned to tread lightly into my mother's room and discovered all the new things she was doing and learning and was constantly amazed. I finally sat down and told her she did have a purpose. It was to teach her "smart-alecky" daughter a lesson! Later that month when I went to visit her I mentioned I was going to have her call an out-of-state friend of hers, but I said I was sorry that I forgot her old address and telephone book at home.

"But you made me a new one!" she said.
"I did?" I asked. *"Where is it?"*
"Right in my drawer down there," she pointed. I looked and there it was.

I sheepishly replied, *"I forgot."* (And secretly said to myself, "Now who is confused, you Smart-aleck, you?")

Now I suppose you are wondering what President Truman has to do with all of this. Well, I did not forget. Here it is:

The President Truman Part
President Truman said:
"It is what you know, after you know it all, that counts!!!"
And he too, along with God and my mother, were exactly right.

Chapter 14

Up the Down Gangplank

One summer weekend during college at my Midwestern university, a friend and I decided to go up to a city in the northern part of the state to see the famous "Blue Angels" flight show. When we arrived, we had to walk quite far from the parking lot down the long dock for the show. We watched and enjoyed the show and then slowly started to walk back when we noticed something. A large ship, lined with sailors, was docked and decorated with red, white and blue ribbons and banners. All the dignitaries from the air show were going up onto the deck. There was the State Attorney General and his wife, the town mayor and other politicians as well as many military dignitaries. We thought it would be very interesting to see the inside of this ship so we headed for the gangplank going up onto the ship. We were immediately stopped since we did not have official passes. Down we went onto the dock again. However, we would not be deterred. We were college students. We were brave, resourceful and ready to buck the system. So we asked ourselves, *"What if we were to get onto ship by going up the down gangplank? Would anyone really tell us not to go up or stop us?"* So we decided we would take a chance. However, we had to prepare for any questioning once we got up there. We cut two rectangles from the program sheet we had and wrote the word "PRESS" on them. He stuck one on his hat and I put one on my sweater pocket. He also had a camera hanging around his neck which made us look even better. We were determined to look official! Over we went to the down gangplank! We waited until there were plenty of people coming down so we would not look so conspicuous going up. Then up we went as fast as we could only to be met by a couple of sailors at the top, who asked us if we were with the official guest party. We feigned confusion about coming onto the ship via the wrong gangplank and pointed to our "PRESS" tags. *"We were in a hurry,"* we said, to *"cover the story of the dignitaries on the ship."* So they let us pass. Now we were really on the ship with the dignitaries. We decided to take some pictures of the water, the view from the deck and the crowds below. Boy, this was good! As we began to approach the lined-up dignitaries, all at once they began to go up the stairs to the very top deck. So we followed them and no one really noticed. Here we were on the top of the ship with all of them. We decided to really push our luck and ask them for a group photo! All smiling, all said they would be glad to since we were from...What newspaper was that again? So we had to actually speak out loud our first untruth! We mumbled *"the Star."* (Well, it sounded almost like the Star and Tribune but we just so happened to leave out the "and Tribune" part. Now they were even more delighted to cooperate and pose for photos. So we lined them up for the photo shoot. The men had on suits and ties or uniforms and the women wore more furs and jewelry than I had ever seen on one person. They all beamed in front of us now, anxious to get their pictures in the paper. Now I became more daring. I thought I should just rearrange them a bit. *"Mr. Attorney General, sir, would you please move over there? Mrs. so-and-so, would you move a little to the right? Admiral, sir, would you please stand in the middle?"* I even went so far as to go over and rearrange the fur piece on the shoulders of the Attorney General's wife. I thought my friend was going to crack-up with laughter, but he held it together. We took a whole roll of film and then asked each one for the correct spelling of their names. We certainly did not want to print their names wrong!

"What day will this be in the paper?" they asked. We uttered something about how we could not be sure. (That was certainly the truth!) The group then was suddenly summoned by some public relations person, to get on the speedboat to tour the shipyard water area. Yes, we were tempted to try to get on the speedboat too. We both had the same thought, then looked at each other, smiled and silently shook our heads no. That would be pushing it and there would be no fast way off a speedboat except jumping into the water and I, for one, could not even

swim. So we ended it. We said our good-byes and thanks, shook hands with all the respected guests and looked for the quickest way off the ship. This time down the down gangplank! We had done it!

We tried to keep our composure all the way back to the car. Smugly we laughed and related the incident over and over again to each other. Then we made a startling discovery! There was no film in the camera! We were in disbelief all the way home. Now we could not even have photos as a souvenir of this occasion! What divine justice this was!

Oh well, it had been a good time anyway. Out of the ordinary and a bit risky but no harm done. And we did not get booted off the ship at least. Anyway we would never see those persons again anyway. Or would we?

Three days later I went to my college classes during the day and then to my part time job in the evening. My job was working in the coat check room at the University Union building, which was used for a lot of public events. At 7 p.m. I turned around and facing me was the Attorney General and his wife wanting their coats checked! I could not run and I could not hide. I just stood there with a ghastly look on my face! When I managed to find my voice I meekly whimpered, *"Check your coats, sir?"* at which time he handed me his overcoat and his wife's fur with the fox eyes which I recognized as being very familiar. Glancing at me for a moment, he asked, *"Have I met you before?"* My answer was, *"Oh no, sir, I am just a student."* And they walked suavely into the conference ballroom and I walked smack into the coat rack! I had to stay there and work for the next three hours until the event was over. It seemed like a week. I kept wondering how I could disguise myself when all the guests picked up their coats. I was sure this was punishment for pulling such a prank. At the end, when the Attorney General and his wife asked for their coats, I moved really, really fast since I had not thought up any way to disguise myself. The last thing the Attorney General did was give me a dollar tip! Now I had to deal with guilt, too, the rest of my life!

That was the last time I ever saw the Attorney General. Many years later, he appeared in a television ad for his law practice. I imagined he was looking right through the television directly at me. I don't expect to ever run into him again but life does play its own tricks on us.

***

And so we all must wait. God wants us to get on his ship of faith now. He does not want us to wait. We don't even need to sneak on. He will let us on board any way we can, either the up or the down gangplank, in any condition, with all of our faults and even full of our irresistible pranks pretending to be something or somebody we are not. How far do we want to go before we accept His hand? God's ship, too, looms at the dock and waits. It is way out of the ordinary, at times even a bit risky, but full of the promise of eternal life. One thing we can count on, like coming face to face with the Attorney General again, we all are destined to come face to face with God again and again. He does not intend to walk away from us, so we might just as well go up the down gangplank now and look forward to a wonderful trip!

Chapter 15

A Nosey Risk

When I was a nursing student in pediatrics (more years ago than I care to remember) I cared for and did a case study on a 6-year-old girl named Judy. She had been on the pediatric unit for a few weeks and she was what some of the staff had labeled a "holy terror." After caring for her for only one day, I understood why. She was one of the most difficult patients I had ever run across. She screamed and yelled and cried at everything and everybody who came near her. She was emotional, impatient, demanding and refused to cooperate in anything without a battle. To tell the truth, I could not come up with any ideas on how to handle her and was at a total loss of what I could do. I really was afraid I would probably flunk pediatrics because of her. When my nursing classmates who had been there the rotation before me found out who my case study patient was, they just rolled their eyes and said, *"Good luck!"*

Judy had a long history of illness and hospitalizations. Stomach malformations prevented her from eating normally, so she had to be fed through a tube every day. She already had been through several operations to try to correct her defects. I did feel sorry for her and felt she probably could not help behaving the way she did. She was an angry little girl. The hospital had moved her from another unit where she was older than the rest of the children. She had terrorized most of the younger children there. Now in this unit she would be one of the youngest. The staff hoped being with older children would improve her behavior. I had my doubts. However, I was getting pretty grumpy myself, not knowing how I was going to bathe her or give her medicine each day without a battle and still keep my sanity. No one could get her to do anything she didn't want to. Even her parents could not talk her into cooperating. She caused such a disturbance that they finally took her out of a three-bed ward with two other children and put her into a room by herself. This still did not change her behavior. It just made for a private spectacle instead of public one.

    I tried everything to coax her into cooperating. I was nice. That didn't work. I was pleasantly firm, which didn't work either. Going into her room every day was getting to be a real challenge, but I didn't want to flunk out of pediatric nursing. I started each day with a nervousness caused by a 6-year-old named Judy. Most of the time I felt like a total failure as a pediatric nurse. I had two more weeks to care for her. I had a feeling it was going to be very miserable for both of us.

    Then came the day things changed. It was the day which in one fleeting moment I decided to take a risk. You can call it foolish. You can call it unprofessional. You might even call it stupid, but I was desperate. Judy had acquired some kind of infection in her sinuses. So her doctor ordered a nose culture. I could not imagine this 6-year-old letting someone stick a culture swab up her nose. The swab was not just a short stick. It was culture swab at the end of a long, and I mean long, wire so it would bend around into the nasal cavity and up to the sinuses. What's more, the pediatrician sent a medical student up to the unit to get the culture. He was a greenhorn, young, shy, nervous, unmarried and had no children. This was going to be both Judy's and my worst nightmare! When the medical student walked into the room carrying the wire culture swab in a big glass tube, Judy's eyes opened wide (and I confess so did mine). She asked him what he was going to do. And he actually told her. I could tell by Judy's face that she thought he was very wrong. He was NOT going to do that! Now what would we do. Now we would be a pair of failures; a medical student who could not even get a nose culture and a student nurse who could not control a 6-year-old patient.

    This was when desperation set in. And before I could stop myself my lips were moving and saying, *"Well, Judy, if I have the doctor do it on me first, will you promise to let him do it on you?"* I think even Judy was shocked or she didn't believe me. She said *"OK"* with what looked to me like a somewhat evil smile. I don't think the medical student could believe it either because he was staring at me in disbelief! I ran out of the room to get another culture set while the two of them stared silently at each other. I returned as fast as I could clutching the extra culture set, before I could change my mind. I was hoping for a miracle and that Judy would change her mind. But this did not happen so I thought I had better get it over with.

It must have been quite a funny scene. The medical student and I standing in front of this 6-year-old with a sly smile on her face, watching me have a wire shoved up my nose. For a moment I thought I maybe had a nervous breakdown. "What on earth was I thinking?" I said to myself as the medical student began pushing the wire culture swab up into my nasal cavity. His hands were shaky and I was putting on a pretty brave front for someone who was experiencing excruciating pain! It was awful and nearly unbearable. But I was an adult and Judy's nurse. I was not about to scream and cry in front of her. When we were done I told Judy (in a much higher and more tense voice than I had before) that it was not too bad and now it was her turn. The medical student and I stared anxiously at her waiting for an outburst. When she said, "OK!", we looked at each other very surprised and then quickly realized that it was now or never. I held Judy while he did the culture. She hardly made a sound (and actually did much better than I did) and we were done quickly. Meanwhile, my nose was screaming with pain and my eyes were burning from holding back the tears. When we got done I praised Judy and quickly retreated to the supply closet, closed the door and let the tears stream down my face. I don't know if it was because of the pain in my nose or just that I was relieved it worked.

After this, Judy and I had a changed relationship. I am not certain what changed in her 6-year-old mind. Did she like me? Probably not. I was still a nurse to her. Did she get a glimpse that I really did care about her? Maybe. I don't think I will ever really know nor do I need to know. All I do know is that I decided to take a risk and it helped. What happened was her behavior became more manageable, she smiled once in a while and we laughed together about our nose cultures!

(However, I silently swore from that moment on, I would never, ever, get another nose culture in my life. And you can bet I have kept that promise to myself!) And I got an A in pediatrics!

***

Once in a while I still run into situations where I am asked or feel like I am being forced to take a risk. It's still challenging, scary and sometimes painful. Risks come in many forms. Like a misbehaving teenager, a new job, a grumpy elderly person, a person who just arrived here from another country, a terminally ill neighbor, an unlikable co-worker, a difficult family member, a task which makes me feel inadequate or a situation that makes me afraid. However, I can think of situations when persons in my life took risks for me. Can we take a risk for someone and always come out like a rose? Probably not. But it could happen. Jesus certainly took all kinds of risks and even death for us. I hope I can keep this in my heart and through His love for me that I can take a few risks for others.

Chapter 16

A Shiny Secret Place

I suppose most people as children had some kind of secret place when they were growing up. A place that they liked to disappear into, be alone and call their own.

When I was five years old my 10-year-old brother had his own room in the basement. He showed movies to his friends on the old movie projector. They laughed at the cartoons and talked about who knows what. I was not allowed to go into his room unless I asked him first and then he had to go in there with me. He thought I might "touch his stuff". (Those were his exact words.) However, that even made it more intriguing to me. Actually my parents informed me of this new "rule" after I had gone into my brother's room several times without permission and looked around when he was not there, just to irritate him. Then my brother tattled on me, so to keep me out, my dad put a hook and eye on the door up high enough so I couldn't reach it. That's when I discovered the value of a wooden yardstick. The yardstick was just long enough to unhook the hook and I could get in the room. Usually when I got in there, I really did not dare "touch his stuff" because if I did I would take a chance that the yardstick might be used for another purpose. But I sure stood there long enough to look at everything. After all, I had to do something to get back at him for all the tricks he played on me. Like giving me peppered gum, trapping me in a snow tunnel or putting dirt in my nice little tea cups.

Then one year something wonderful happened. My dad got a new job as a state bus line driver. And what I got was a shiny secret place.

It was very long, had lots of windows and lots of seats. It was a shiny bus. In the moonlight of this small town without street lights, the silver colored sides of the bus would nearly glow in the dark. My dad would bring the bus home when he had to leave early the next morning and would park it right in front of our house. So one of my brother's and my favorite places to play was in the bus. In fact, we had many battles about playing in the bus. So many that my Dad made us take turns each night. So when my brother was playing somewhere with his friends, I would sneak into the bus without him knowing it and have the time of my life. I was proud of myself because I knew where the secret button was on the front of the bus that popped open the door. When I used to ride with my dad through the small towns on his bus route, it was always fascinating to me that he would let the passengers off the bus to eat lunch, then he and I would get off the bus, close the door and everybody had to wait until he came back to pop the secret button to open the door.

  I loved my new shiny secret place. In the dark I would run up and down the aisles, sit in the driver's seat, sing out loud to myself, sit in every passenger seat and talk to imaginary travelers pretending I was traveling to all kinds of places. It was wonderful! Well, almost always wonderful. There were a few times when I had crept up to the door of the bus, looked around for my brother to make sure he was not in sight, then quickly pushed the secret button to open the bus door and happily climb into the bus, only to discover that my brother had gotten in there before me and was hiding in the luggage rack above the seats. He would scream and scare me to death. Otherwise, it was a grand shiny secret place! To this day I am still kind of fascinated by buses. Whenever I end up going on some kind of a bus tour, I confess, I always manage to sneak a peek at the front to see where the secret button is. The last time I was on a shuttle bus at some event, I even got the nerve up to ask the driver if there was still that secret button on the front of the bus. There was.

***

I guess we all try to find a secret place. A place where we can just be ourselves with no false pretenses, no pressure to be ahead, no acting self-assured all the time, no people messing with "our stuff." A place

I Thought There Was a Road There

where we can just quickly pop the secret button and get in and be alone in the dark. Everyone probably needs a secret place. I figure even though I am no longer six years old and fighting with my brother I can still manage to have that secret place because God can provide it. He knows who I really am and who I am not. The real me is not always brave, self-assured, strong, positive and never doubting, but someone who needs help sometimes. I do not have to be perfect in my secret place because God still accepts me as I am with my faults, with my sins, with my doubt and with my questions.

This too, is a grand secret place to be!

Chapter 17

Making It Complicated When It Is Not!

There are times in my life when I have found myself making things complicated when they didn't need to be. I am about to confess some of them.

There was the time when my husband and I bought our first new car. We had been married about eight years but could never afford a new car. Excited, we drove the new car home with those paper license plates in the window. Some days later, we picked up the real license plates. Then armed with our screwdriver, we walked out to the street where our new car was parked in front of our house. It should have been simple to put a couple of license plates on! Right? Wrong! As the sun set in the west we were still trying to get those license plates on. My husband was sweating and sitting on the ground and I was holding the flashlight in the dark so he could see where the teeny, tiny license plate holes were. Finally we succeeded and got those license plates on. About a week later, I was talking to my Dad and was telling him what an awful ordeal it was to try to do this in the dark with only a flashlight. My Dad paused and asked,

"Don't you have a garage?"
"Yes," I said.
"Well, does it have a light in it?" he asked.
"Yes," I said.
"Well, why didn't you just drive it in the garage and put the plates on there?"

Then I remember when recycling became mandatory. We MUST recycle and MUST learn recycling regulations. Recycling began to rule our lives. I read the rules in the paper over and over: newspapers separate, business (white paper only) separate, plastic (certain numbers that is) separate, pop cans who knows where and glass not at all, I think.

People in town were rushing to the stores to get the "proper" recycling containers. And I was right along with them. I did not want to get fined or have my garbage pile up because I was not recycling correctly. Every store had hundreds of recycling bins stacked outside so we all could buy enough. I remember standing outside of the store with about a dozen other panicky women looking at all the yellow, blue and green recycling tubs. Women were grabbing one of each color and then asking every other woman, "Which is for paper? Which is for metal? Which is for plastic?" In our crazed minds we actually thought we had to have a certain color and nobody knew which color was correct for what. So we all bought one of each color since there were three different colors. We all frantically grabbed at the yellow ones, because they seemed to be going fast. After paying, we all walked to our cars and loaded our wares. We were now officially in the recycling world! And proud of it.

So that day I spent organizing the entire house for recycling. I made labels on my computer to put on the colored bins (hoping I assigned the right colors to the right item) and then neatly lined the containers up in the garage. Of course, then we had to have all kinds of bins and containers in the house. Some upstairs, downstairs and in the basement so we could keep things sorted inside in order to take them outside. That was it! I was finished and now we could recycle properly. And so we did for several years. The trouble is those funny-shaped containers with their flimsy lids drove us crazy. First of all, they had no actual handles. Then when the garbage man emptied them, he stuck them all inside each other and we had to pull them apart. And the nice labels I made got wet when it rained and the printing smeared so I had to put plastic tape over the labels. The lids got cracked and bent and never fit right and sometimes the wind blew them away all over the yard.

Then one day I came to my senses. I asked myself, *"Was there ever really a mandated color to recycling bins?* I don't think so. *Was there a law that said they have to be covered?"* I doubted it, but I would call to find out. Then I had the most remarkable conclusion. If there does not have to be a cover, and there are not assigned "colors" to recycling tubs, then why do I need these complicated containers? It was so simple and I had made it so complicated! So the next day, I went out and bought three same-size, same-color plastic tubs with no covers and nice big rope handles on each side. I did not even need signs. It was sort of like kindergarten all over again, putting similar things together. I was finally at peace with recycling.

***

Sometimes it is the same with God's love. We tend to make it so complicated. We worry about what we have to do to be near perfect human beings. We look at other people and judge them. We try to figure out how many good deeds we have done, how nice we have been to others, how much we have given to others less fortunate, how many hours we have spent working for charity, how much money we have donated to good causes, blah, blah, blah.

Not that these things are bad. They are good, but this is not God's point! Because what does God really ask of us? To be famous? To be perfect? To be outstanding? To be popular? To do a good deed every day? No, not really. All He asks for is our true faith and love; and maybe to remember...not to make things too complicated...when they are not!

Chapter 18

Taking It From the Top...like "Tigger"

In the 1970s we had moved to California and decided to get a dog. We only paid five dollars for our shy, black puppy who the kids named Tigger (from Winnie the Pooh stories). As Tigger got used to us and we to him, he became like another child in the family. For the next 13 years we got to know his habits and quirks as well as we knew each other. He was what we called an "outside dog". This meant that outside was his usual habitat since it was sunny California. He really seemed to love life and watched everything which happened around him like the birds, bees, and butterflies, yard lizards and anything which moved.

Then one day he made a discovery. If he took a big enough leap, he could stand on the top of his doghouse, difficult as it might be (it had a pointed roof) and he could see even more of the world. There happened to be a small tree just beside his doghouse so he would place his front paws on one branch of the tree to prop himself up just a little higher. He would spend the greater part of each day on the roof of his doghouse observing everything and anything. Of course, he took breaks for eating, sleeping, taking naps or playing with the children. However, he never liked to sleep in the doghouse. He just climbed on top of it. All night he would sleep outside on the grass. It was good that it didn't rain much because he slept outside rain or shine.

Then came the day when we moved back to the Midwest. What was Tigger to do? He was an "outside" dog. We supposed we would have to let him be an "inside" dog now. However, Tigger was so used to being outside that he couldn't stand to be inside.

He whined and whined and we knew he wanted to be outside most of the time. So we fenced the yard, had a large dog kennel built, bought an insulated dog house and let him return to being an "outside" dog once again. It was very evident he was happy in his "outside" kingdom and pranced around as if he were royalty. He would come and look at us through the glass patio door but didn't want to come in. He was just checking on us I guess. When we did let him in, he would soon start whining so we would let him out again. It was as if things were happening out there and he did not want to miss anything. We suspected he would change his mind when the severe Midwest winters hit, but he did not. He still romped around in the snow, sometimes catching snowflakes in his mouth and chasing gray rabbits around the drifts. And he still climbed on top of the doghouse to see what else was happening. He refused to sleep in his doghouse even in the dead of winter. We put a piece of carpet over the door so the wind wouldn't get in. We stuffed a nice huge old quilt inside his dog house so he would keep warm. But Tigger dragged the quilt slowly and methodically straight out of the doghouse door and onto the biggest snow drift in the yard. Then he slept on top of the quilt! I will never forget looking out one dark winter night and seeing Tigger on that quilt covered with snow. Tigger stayed healthy for some years and then got what was called "heartworm." We had to give him medicine and confine him to just the small area inside his kennel to protect his heart condition. His medical treatment was costly. We now had a $500 dog! But Tigger still romped around his kennel and stood on top of his doghouse for endless hours. We would go in the kennel and play and "visit" him. The boys would sit on top of the doghouse with him. After his three-month medical confinement was complete, we got to let him out of his kennel and he ran prancing all over the yard again! He had not changed a bit.

It wasn't until he was about 12 years old that his health deteriorated. He developed arthritis, cataracts and bladder problems. We were willing to let him stay in the house now, but he just couldn't stand being inside. He wanted to be outside even though he was nearly blind, miserable, shivering and struggling to walk. He couldn't even manage to climb on top of his doghouse anymore. It was a sad day when we had to make the decision to have him "put to sleep" so he would not be miserable anymore. But I think he is probably romping around in "dog heaven" somewhere and has found the biggest, highest cloud there to climb on top of and literally have the best view he ever had of the rest of the world.

We learned a lot about life from Tigger. He never gave up hope. He always seemed to be happy. He kept his independence as long as he possibly could. He wanted to be where the action was. He faced headlong into bad weather. If confined, he made the best of it. He got pleasure out of simple things. He found excitement in an ordinary day in an ordinary yard. He never gave up. He lived life on top (of his dog house, that is).

***

God tells us these same things in so many ways. Be a part of the world and observe its beauty and events. Never give up hope and enjoy life as it happens.

We need to face headlong into life's situations because God is always beside us. Simple lives are OK to have because all we really need is faith. We can be ordinary people in ordinary lives and God will never forsake us and will always give us His love. We, too, need to take it from the top like Tigger!

Chapter 19

Life After the Carnival

When I was an eight-year old, we lived in a small town. I thought our house was in the best part of town. (In reality, it was the poorest part of town, but I didn't know it.) The reason I loved our neighborhood was because it was just a half a block from the fairgrounds. The fairgrounds had lots of things going on, especially in the summer like stock car races, farm equipment shows, carnivals and fairs. My parents never allowed me at that age to go the fairs or carnivals by myself. They said it was too dangerous. Of course, I didn't believe them at all. The fairgrounds was such a fun place. There was music, Ferris wheels and other wonderful rides, flashing lights, all kinds of food and lots of those smiling people who worked at the fair. You know, the ones who keep saying, *"Come on in! Win the big prize! You can do it! Try your luck! Only one thin dime!"* My parents called them "carnies" and said it could be dangerous over there. I somehow got the idea my parents thought I might be kidnapped and whisked away to travel with the "carnies" all over the country for the rest of my life. Sounded kind of adventurous to me! But since I usually tried to obey my parents, I never even tried to sneak over to the carnivals and fairs by myself even though my brother who was 5 years older than me got to go with his friends. I guess I was just a little scared too.

    The carnivals and fairs were really lots of fun when my parents took me. But secretly I could not wait until the carnival left town. Because now came the best part. Once the carnival was gone then I and my friends could go to the fairgrounds by ourselves. We could go there and wander around and find all kinds of things left over from the carnival and the people. The only thing was we had to beat my brother and his friends there, so I never told my brother when we were going. Life after the carnival was so exciting! We found all kinds of surprises! Like money people had dropped. Or prizes that had been lost! It was like a treasure hunt. We would walk around the entire fairgrounds and find all kinds of things! No music, no lights and no rides and no "carnies." It was safe! And we could explore and imagine what was there before. So off we went each year after the carnival and had such fun.

***

Our lives too are sometimes like those carnivals. Full of music, adventure, lots of people, a few prizes, bright lights and lots of noise and entertainment. It seems like the ultimate place to be. What could possibly beat this? God offers us much more after our carnival of life. He offers us more than we can even imagine! There is no admission price, no special openings, no prizes, and anyone is accepted. And all He asks is that we believe and have faith. We need to accept this with open arms and hearts to enter into the carnival of heaven and everlasting life!

Chapter 20

Ducks, Ducks Everywhere

It seems throughout all of my life I keep running into ducks. Ducks are all right I guess and fun to watch, but I don't especially like them more than other animals. I have only ordered duck once in a restaurant. I don't know how to cook duck. I have never been educated on different kinds of ducks. Yet, ducks keep popping up into my life.

The first time was in high school when I was a writer for our high school paper. I had to think of something unusual and entertaining to write about. So the idea came to me. It was fall and my neighbor was going duck hunting. Never having experienced this, I decided to go along and then write about it from a female perspective.

What a mistake that was! We got up in the middle of the night and rode out into the wilderness. Crouched among wet weeds, cattails and thistles in the dark we all waited. I kept asking where the ducks were and the hunters kept telling me to be quiet and they would show up. What seemed like hours later, the ducks did show up. And then they got shot! It was not my kind of sport. I decided I was not in favor of duck hunting. In fact, once when my mother fixed duck for supper I took a bite and got a mouth full of buckshot. I vowed to never to be a part of duck hunting again!

Many years later my husband was a resident in his surgical training, and once again I had to deal with ducks. He was doing experiments on duck pancreases to study aspects of diabetes. He would have to spend late nights in the laboratory watching how the ducks reacted to certain medications and then do blood tests on them every two hours. If there were only one or two ducks left to watch he would decide to bring the ducks home in their cages and put them in our basement. Then he could at least get some sleep in between drawing blood. (I got my choice on how to help. I could either hold the wing or draw the blood. I held the wing!) If the duck happened to die in the night he would have to put the duck in our freezer so an autopsy could be done on the duck the next morning. Several times, I got up in the morning, only to open the freezer and see two webbed feet sticking out!

Several years ago I started a new job in a building with an enclosed atrium with a lot of plants and trees. I was told that each year a duck flew into the atrium and laid eggs. Since it was surrounded by walls, when the baby ducks hatched and could not yet fly, we had to be ready to open up the doors to allow the mother and ducklings to walk to the nearby lake. And so the first year I was there, I was privileged to help the mother and babies walk right through our carpeted classroom through the open door to the outside, stop the traffic so the ducks could cross the street to go the two blocks to the lake and follow them to make sure they got there safely. Now that was truly a good duck experience that I will never forget!

Some years later, my company moved to a new building without an area suitable for ducks, so I did not encounter ducks for a while. But then, when we had our company out-of-state annual meeting, I got a reminder that duck sightings were not over yet. I had just climbed on a large bus with many other people and we were waiting to go on a tour. It seemed like we were all there and all the other buses had left but ours. So I wondered what was holding us up? I looked out the window. Of course, there was a big duck slowly crossing the road in front of the bus, and taking his time, so the bus couldn't start out.

A few years later, our company building expanded into three buildings, much landscaping and a nice little lake. You guessed it! Ducks were once again back into my daily life.

On my way to work, I would pass that small lake and look over and see not one, not two, but several ducks sunning, swimming, and taking care of their baby ducks. I guess I had better stop being surprised any more at duck encounters. That is just the way it will be from now on. I had better get used to it.

Then one year I had major surgery and was away from work for six weeks. I was so glad to get back to work, and as I wound my way down the road and drove next to the quiet, shining still water, I almost longed to see a duck. And when I did, I felt at home!

***

These duck encounters which I did not expect remind me of something else in my life that I forget to expect. That God too shows up when I think He will not. He enters my life when I don't expect it but when I need it and is always nearby even if I fail to recognize this. He crosses my path when I am wondering why things are not going the way I think they should. I need those reminders, those sightings of God, encounters with my faith, because though I do not always deserve His attention, I can still always count on it.

Chapter 21

That was Enough of That!

When I was a small child of about 7 or 8, my mother decided I should learn some kind of craft, so she chose embroidery for me. One day at my aunt's house, she brought along a dishtowel and embroidery materials and taught me how to do some stitches. I was sitting on my aunt's porch dutifully embroidering away (but not liking it much) when my mother came out to check on how I was doing. *"See,"* I said, to show her what I had done. As I lifted up the dishtowel on my lap, my dress came up with it! I had embroidered my dishtowel to the skirt of my dress. That was enough of that!

Upon entering high school, students were invited to high school choir try-outs. I liked music and thought it might be fun. I never really sang with a choir before except in our small church choir, but some of my friends were trying out. So I went, too. We had to sit next to the choir director at the piano and sing a scale and then sing from some sheet music. While I was sitting there (petrified, I might add), he called my name and I had to approach the piano. I looked at the choir director and then looked at the sheet music and turned pale. He asked me to sing a scale. My mouth opened but no sound would come out. No choir for me that year. Maybe next year, he said. That was enough of that!

One time when I was in my late twenties, I was visiting my father. He did all his own work on his cars and he thought it would be good for me to learn to change the oil in my own car and not have to pay anyone to do this. "It was so simple," he said. So he gave me verbal instructions. All I needed to do was to crawl under my car, taking with me something to use as an oil pan. Then unscrew the oil plug, or bolt, or whatever he called it, to drain the oil. Just let the oil drain, replace the plug and it would be all done. Then all I would have to do was add new oil. I agreed. Sure, it would be good for me to learn this and it would save money! So a few months later, I got some kind of a pan to drain the oil into, crawled under my car, (after of course laying down a blanket on the garage floor,) and searched for the oil plug. Success! I found it and was staring right at it when one tiny drop of oil dripped onto my cheek. I immediately was repulsed and got myself out from under the car and vowed never to attempt it again. That was enough of that.

In my thirties, I decided I would try my hand at oil painting. After all, Grandma Moses started later than that. I went to the art store and got tubes of oil paint, brushes, a palate and a nice piece of canvas. My first oil painting. What would it be? A person? No, I don't think I should start with people right away. An animal? Not really because they still have limbs, and bodies and eyes and such. I had better practice a while first. I decided on a tree. A tree would be simple, just leaves and branches. That would be easy enough. So I painted away, painting the trunk then the leaves. Maybe I would even attempt a bird nesting in the tree. But as I painted, it seemed my paint brush had other ideas. When I tried to paint lines for the tree trunk, it was an awful smudged line! When I tried to paint the leaves it looked like a mess of green paint instead of leaves! I tried different brushes but they behaved no better than the rest. How on earth did Grandma Moses do this? Well, I decided I was a miserable failure at oil painting and should probably just go back to kindergarten and start over with crayons.

And again, That was enough of that!

***

There are more instances of my failures which I could talk about. I am not good at athletics, chess or flower gardening. But at least now after all these years I do know what I am good at. And I try to stick with those things and steer clear of the others. In our Christian lives it would be wonderful to be able to say "That was enough of that!" whenever we want or need to. Like when we tend to criticize others, gossip, lean towards dishonesty, put too much importance on material things in life, avoid helping others who are less fortunate, or forget that faith in God should be our focus. This is when I wish the elbow of God would just give me a little nudge...and say *"That is enough of that!"*

Chapter 22

Messages I Did Not Want to Get

Some of the messages we used to receive from our sons when they were growing up were certainly a cause for parental dismay. Usually we had to attempt to decipher what they really meant, since they only gave enough information to throw us into a panic. It became a difficult task to imagine the rest of the story or what was not being explained.

For instance, there was the time one of our sons borrowed the car and drove with a friend of his to a nearby college, an hour and a half away, to see his friend's sister. That was all right, I thought. No harm in that. He promised to have the car back by 6 or 7 p.m. Yes, I was naive. It could not possibly be that simple. And at 5 p.m. the message on the answering machine was, *"Hi, Mom, I might be a little late. We went fishing with the Iranians."*

Then there was one fall quarter when one of our sons went off to college and after arriving in his college dorm room left the following message: *"I haven't seen my roommate yet, but he must be moved in because his spiked dog collar and chains and green hair dye are in the closet."*

Another time we received a phone message from another son which said, *"Hi mom, I will call you later. I just want to talk to you about my condition."* (I was faster than a speeding bullet trying to call him back!)

Time and time again ambiguous messages crept into our household –

"I am in town, I will call you sometime."
"I am home. The car is not."
"I am at a friend's house, we are staying in the attic."

There were perfectly good explanations behind all of these messages once I was able to get the rest of the story. However, in the meantime, we had to wait and wait and imagine the worst situations. Just for your information here are the explanations:

"Fishing with the Iranians." The friend's sister, had met some Iranian students at the college, and they had never fished. So they took them fishing at the lake.

"The roommate with the spiked dog collar and chains and green hair dye." Yes, he was a punk rocker but actually was a very nice person. Turned out though this particular part of the dorm was much too quiet so he moved to another part of the dorm which was more suited to him.

The son with the *"condition"*. It was not a disease. He simply was being funny and meant his monetary condition. He needed money.

"I am in town, I will call you sometime." This was related to the fact that he had a new girlfriend in town and we did not know until he decided to tell us later. We thought it was strange he was coming home from college, (a 5 hour drive) more often than usual.

"I am home. The car is not." He ran out of gas just a few blocks away but he was tired so he walked home and left the car where it was.

"We are staying in the attic." His friend had one of those rooms upstairs that used to be an attic and was recently remodeled into a bedroom.

***

In our lives we all get messages which we do not want or understand about illness or death of a loved one, divorce, disruption of our best plans and changes to our future. Which is why life is so hard at times. We get messages of *"I love you"* and then actions which do not quite fit. We get messages of *"I will take care of it"* and then nothing happens. We get messages of *"I need you"* and then we are never asked. We get messages of *"I am sorry"* and then we get repeated offenses. These messages are difficult to receive and may cause us to be insecure and unhappy.

God also gives us messages. But do we always listen to these? We may want to follow our own instincts and our own wishes. God's message is simple. He loves us and wants us beside Him! There are no demands for perfection, no special deeds, no complicated rules, no further explanations. We just need to have faith. That's all He asks while he gives us the ultimate message, *"Have no fear. I am with you always."* It is a simple message but we continue to struggle with it. And I imagine we will always struggle with it. That is why we need to cling to our faith and continue the struggle. For in the end this is the only message that really counts!

Epilogue

What kinds of roads did you travel on yesterday? Or the day before? Or last month or last year? Were there lessons learned on those roads? Let us hope no matter which direction we travel as we trudge along our roads of life, real or imaginary, we still allow God to travel beside us. And if once in a while we mistakenly happen to think "THERE IS A ROAD THERE!" and find ourselves around the bend, or at the fork, on the freeway or the back road, let us know and hope that God is surely right beside us.

www.ingramcontent.com/pod-product-compliance
Lightning Source LLC
LaVergne TN
LVHW051217070526
838200LV00063B/4933